W9-BFM-847

...and The Pursuit of HAPPINESS

All rights reserved. No part of this book may be used in any manner without the written permission of the publisher, unless you have a very good reason for doing so without such permission. Best of Faith to you, my Friend!

Published by JIC Enterprises
Boston, Massachusetts

ISBN-13: 978-1548161316
ISBN-10: 1548161314

First Edition ©June 2017
This Edition ©January 2018

For more information please visit
www.JonasCain.com

ABOUT THE AUTHOR

Jonas Cain is a positivity expert, author, magician, and corporate trainer. For over twenty years he has sought to engage, empower, and encourage others to become Positivity Leaders at home, work, and within the community.

Through his interactive keynote presentations, motivational magic performances, and engaging training workshops, Jonas has worked with major corporations, organizations, universities, sporting teams, military installations, and countless individuals, sharing research, tools, and strategies for developing and fostering positivity in all areas of life.

For complete information on his programs, or if you'd like to invite Jonas to speak with your group, visit:

www.JonasCain.com

READER REVIEWS OF JONAS CAIN'S BOOKS

A LIFE-Changing Book!

By <u>Leah</u> on January 3, 2012

"It Just Happened the Other Day is an 'I can't put it down book and let me read it again!!!' It has life, love, joy, sadness, beginning and endings — truly a book for young and old. It is a book that has to touch one's heart and open one's life to what "love" is truly about! It is an easy read but has great depth!! A great gift for anyone!!! The best gift to yourself. It is life changing!!"

He Does Everything With Passion!

By <u>Liane Muise</u> on November 5, 2016

"The story he shared was a very personal one. It was inspirational. He exposed something he experienced in his life to show his readers that even when you face the darkest times that there is always a reason to forge ahead. I could connect with his words and it was well worth every page. Jonas is an incredible writer, magician and overall just a great person. Everything he does he does with passion and you will not be disappointed if you decide to read his book or attend one of his shows."

Rediscovery of How to Live!

By <u>Vulcanicus</u> on December 11, 2012

"This book contains all the required principles for living a happy life. It draws from a variety of excellent sources to instruct the reader in achieving their goals. I highly recommend you read and ponder it as a fine wine being tasted and enjoyed for the first time."

Well Expressed Emotion
By <u>Cari S.</u> on October 22, 2012

"From the first page, I was hooked. The author expressed such great love and true emotion. A tender and tragic story. Thank you for sharing your heart!"

The Right Information!
By <u>Julie</u> on March 26, 2012

"We all have tough times and everyone handles it differently. Jonas chose to use his experience to help others. This book came to me at an opportune moment. I just finished Making Things Happen, by Cathy Sticker, and this book picked up where I was left. Nicely done, Jonas. Keep up the good work!"

Truly Inspirational!
By <u>Heather Neal</u> on April 13, 2015

"Incredibly empowered by this book. His spirit and love of life is truly inspirational. Highly recommend this book to anyone. Great short read!"

Amazing!
By <u>Jeff</u> on September 19, 2012

"Probably the best book I ever read in a long time, for the stories, the horror, the laughs, the tears, and for the slaps to the heads. This is a book every human on this earth should read and experience what it is like to live."

A Great and Inspiring Book!
By <u>R.B. Carroll</u> on January 2, 2012

"Get this book! It is a fun read with interesting stories and real life events that will inspire you to make the most of your life."

1/25/18

For You

Lauren —

May your pursuit be filled
with Joy! Thank you for
The support.

Peace —

CONTENTS

Jonas Cain off the coast of Kauai — September 7, 2016

CHAPTER ONE
PURSUING HAPPINESS

"To live would be an awfully big adventure."

— Peter Banning

PURSUING HAPPINESS

I don't make decisions lightly but, when I do, I go all in. Like the time I went on a bicycle ride: I got rid of all of my possessions, sold my car, quit my job, and gave up my apartment. My intent was to go cross-country and I didn't want the luxury of being able to fall back on giving up to go back home. By ridding myself of a home I had few options but to move forward.

That said, I never did made it cross-country on the bicycle, but where the ride brought me was to a chiseled sculpture of who I want to be. It is still yet to be fully defined, but I can now see features that once lay dormant beneath the uncut stone of my character. There are many rough edges, and I'll admit that they are often painful to smooth out, but I now see a "me" that I never knew before. That is the reward for Pursuing Happiness.

This book outlines various philosophical theories of happiness along with examples from my own life attempting to live by those philosophies. It's my hope that what you find here will help illuminate your own pursuit, or at the very least expand your knowledge and understanding.

I made this undertaking for three reasons:

1) To better understand my own view of happiness.

2) To communicate some of the various popular theories of happiness in an attempt to offer clarity.

3) To help myself and others live happier lives.

Perhaps the hardest part of this endeavor is the part about seeking to communicate.

THE PROBLEM OF COMMUNICATION

What animal do you see on the previous page? Do you see a duck? Or do you see a rabbit? The playwright Bernard Shaw once said that the biggest problem with communication is the illusion that it has taken place. And haven't we all experienced that? We might find ourselves in a situation where we fully *believe* that we communicated *something* to someone, but this other person's behavior, words, and actions prove otherwise. Because it turns out there was never any communication after all, only the illusion that it had taken place.

I'm reminded of the story of a husband and wife, who were enjoying a romantic evening together sitting under the stars. The husband looked at his wife and said:

"You know, honey, in the moonlight your teeth look just like pearls."

Responding to this beautiful sentiment the wife turned to her husband and said: "Who the heck is Pearl? And what were you doing with her in the moonlight?!"

As this suggests, communication can be difficult when everyone is not on the same page, but it's especially difficult when some people aren't even reading from the same book!

There's a common excuse that says:

"I'm only responsible for what I say, not for what you understand."

But this maxim is just an excuse and not a valid reason to allow confusion to linger. Responsible individuals, teams, leaders, and communities understand that it's everyone's responsibility, as individuals and as group units, to ensure that understanding takes place. This is cannot be a solo effort; for understanding to take place there must by definition be at least two parties involved:

1) The one communicating, and
2) The one being communicated to.

If one of these parties isn't committed to being open and charitable — that is, meeting the other where he or she is — then genuine understanding will not take place and therefore communication will not take place.

Coming from this perspective, I aim to be charitable with some of the more popular theories of happiness from throughout recorded history, using a line written by Thomas Jefferson as a starting point.

THOMAS JEFFERSON

In the Declaration of Independence Thomas Jefferson wrote:

> *"We hold these truths to be self-evident, that all men are created equal, that they are endowed by their*

> *Creator with certain unalienable Rights, that among these are Life, Liberty and the pursuit of Happiness."*[1]

Focusing on the last five words: *"and the pursuit of Happiness,"* and assuming that this statement is true, the question becomes:

> *What exactly is this "happiness" that we have a fundamental right to pursue?*

The contemporary understanding of happiness seems to often focus on "pleasant," "positive" emotions, and having one's needs met; however in 1776 the common meaning may very well have meant "prosperity," "thriving," and "wellbeing."

THEORIES OF HAPPINESS

To understand the intention behind this word we will begin Chapter One by examining the author himself, which will quickly bring us to a discussion of an ancient Greek philosopher and the roots of *hedonism* — a theory of happiness that favors felt sensations of pleasure. In Chapter Two we will discuss both *quantitative* and *qualitative* hedonism, and in Chapter Three we will outline *attitudinal* hedonism, which favors happiness as a mental or psychological sensation of pleasure.

In Chapter Four will discuss *eudemonism* — a theory that believes happiness is achieved by living

---

[1] Jefferson, Thomas. *The Declaration of Independence.* 1776

a life of virtue to live an excellent human life by fulfilling our full potential.

In Chapter Five will discuss *life satisfactionism* — a theory that believes happiness is achieved when we are overall satisfied with our lives as a whole, based on actually occurring pleasures even if pains find their way into our lives.

Lastly, in Chapter Six we will end our formal discussion of happiness with my own personal prescription for living a happy life with in an essay called *The Structure of Happiness*. This dissertation stands on the shoulders of the philosophies revealed in this book, and is measured by my personal application of them in my own pursuit of happiness. It is my belief that the model discussed in this section is both objective and subjective, in that the structure is sound universally, yet must be applied to one's own life to be effective.

A journey of discovery awaits...let us begin!

CHAPTER TWO

HEDONISM

Is It Really All About Pleasure?

"Hunger for hope may be worse than hunger for food."

— Jacob Heym

HEDONISM

There is some debate among scholars as to what inspired Thomas Jefferson to include the phrase "...and the pursuit of Happiness" in the Declaration of Independence, however what is known is that Jefferson was a self-proclaimed Epicurean.

EPICURUS

Epicureanism is a school of philosophy founded in 307 BC that is based on the teachings of the ancient Greek philosopher Epicurus. This ancient philosopher believed that pleasure was the greatest good.[2] The emphasis on pleasure makes Epicurus a hedonist, however his understanding of pleasure does not focus on the lower quality pleasures, such as those of the body; rather, it is focused on the higher quality pleasures, such as those attained through the acquisition of knowledge, by living modestly, and limiting one's desires. By seeking to derive the greatest amount of higher quality pleasure Epicurus believed this to be the path to tranquility and freedom from fear, which once attained lead to happiness.

It's important to note that according to Epicurus, the acquisition of knowledge was sought

---

[2] Pursuit-of-Happiness.org/History-of-Happiness/Epicurus

only to rid oneself of the fear of Gods and of the fear of death. As such, Epicurus' philosophy did not advocate a belief in God. Since Jefferson was a self-proclaimed Epicurean, it is a safe conclusion that he likewise did not advocate for the belief in God. What supports this inference is that while it is known that he was an avid reader of the Christian Bible, he also created his own version, which he called *The Life and Morals of Jesus of Nazareth.*[3] Today this text is often simply referred to as *The Jefferson Bible.* This adaptation removed all mention of Jesus' miracles, and rather only depicts him as a teacher of morals.

What this might suggest, then, is that Jefferson's use of the phrase *"and the pursuit of happiness"* had nothing to do with Epicurus. Notice the reference to a Creator (with a capital "C"):

> *"We hold these truths to be self-evident, that all men are created equal, that they are endowed by their* <u>*Creator*</u> *with certain unalienable Rights..."*

With his personal (subjective) deemphasize on God, perhaps Jefferson's intention here was to create a universal (objective) direction for the citizens of the emerging new nation.

JOHN LOCKE

---

[3] Jefferson, Thomas. *The Life and Morals of Jesus of Nazareth.* 1895

A possible answer can be found with John Locke, a seventeenth century English philosopher who coined the phrase "pursuit of happiness" eighty-seven years before the Declaration of Independence was written. The phrase was used in his book *An Essay Concerning Human Understanding*, and so perhaps an understanding of Locke's view on happiness will bring us closer to understanding our pursuit.

> *"The necessity of pursuing happiness [is] the foundation of liberty. As therefore the highest perfection of intellectual nature lies in a careful and constant pursuit of true and solid happiness; so the care of ourselves, that we mistake not imaginary for real happiness, is the necessary foundation of our liberty. The stronger ties we have to an unalterable pursuit of happiness in general, which is our greatest good, and which, as such, our desires always follow, the more are we free from any necessary determination of our will to any particular action."* [4]

What's important to note in Locke's view of happiness is the distinction between "real" and "imagined" happiness, which suggests an objective view of happiness rather than a subjective one. For example, you may have a strong desire to indulge in rich chocolate cake, and you may believe that indulging in this urge will bring you pleasure, but

---

[4] Locke, John. *An Essay Concerning Human Understanding*. 1689 — ch. 21 §51

Locke would argue that this is only imagined pleasure and not really in your best interest — he would try to convince you that rich chocolate cake will not lead to a "true and solid" happiness that is required for satisfaction with life, since such indulgences are only temporary rather than lasting sources of happiness. Put another way: if you place your happiness inside of a sand castle then you will lose your happiness every time the tide comes in. But if you instead place your happiness where neither moth nor rust can destroy[5] then your happiness will be true and solid.

John Locke's "unalterable pursuit of happiness" advocates for a freedom to make decisions that would result in the best life possible for a human being, however this does not imply that we should be at liberty to choose anything *less* than that which would lead to true and solid happiness. Therefore, if Thomas Jefferson was inspired by Locke then this could insinuate, to use an extreme and absurd example, a ban on the production and sale of rich chocolate cakes, because choosing such base pleasures would not lead to genuine happiness. This is an extreme example, but consider the implication of Locke's theory: we have the right to pursue happiness by being free to choose that which would lead to "true and solid," long-lasting happiness. By including rich chocolate cake in our

---

[5] Matthew 6:20

mix of choices, it is not in keeping with the spirit of Locke's understanding of happiness, because making such a choice would lead only to a fleeting pleasure that lasts only until the next tide comes in.

JEREMY BENTHAM

The eighteenth-century British philosopher Jeremy Bentham would likely disagree with such a proposition, and if you find fault with this interpretation of Locke's happiness, perhaps Bentham's ideas will be more convincing.

Bentham was a quantitative hedonist, believing that happiness is a singular, measurable, felt sensation of pleasure.[6] Because of his emphasis on measuring *quantity* of pleasure, he took no consideration for the *quality* of pleasure. To be happy by Bentham's theory, then, is simply a matter of experiencing a greater quantity of pleasure over pain or neutral states.

To support this claim he argued that every felt sensation either offers a measure of pleasure or a measure of pain. Modern philosophers call these measures "hedons" and "dolors," with a hedon being a measure of pleasure and a dolor being a

---

[6] Mulnix, Jennifer Wilson; Mulnix, M.J. *Happy Lives, Good Lives: A Philosophical Examination.* Broadview Press, 2015 — p. 62

measure of pain.[7] Think of a hedon as a positive measure (+) and a dolor as a negative measure (–). In this way, the sum total of one's hedons and dolors is the measure of one's happiness.

Bentham suggested seven criteria for quantifying pleasure:

1) **Intensity:** *The intensity of the pleasure or pain.*

2) **Duration:** *How long the pleasure or pain will last.*

3) **Certainty:** *The probability that the event will be pleasurable or painful.*

4) **Propinquity/Remoteness:** *How soon will the event occur.*

5) **Fecundity:** *The probability of the pleasure leading to further pleasure.*

6) **Purity:** *The probability of the pain leading to further pain.*

7) **Extant:** *The number of individuals to be effected by the pleasure or pain.*

To understand how to use this criteria, let's consider the pleasure derived from a hypothetical game of chess to the pleasure derived from a hypothetical game of Russian roulette:

---

[7] Mulnix, Jennifer Wilson; Mulnix, M.J. *Happy Lives, Good Lives: A Philosophical Examination.* Broadview Press, 2015 — p. 65

1) **Intensity:** It's safe to infer that Russian roulette will be the far more intense activity versus chess, therefore Russian roulette would be deemed more pleasurable.

2) **Duration:** Chess can sometimes last for hours and hours, whereas Russian roulette can end almost immediately, making it a rather short-lived endeavor. Therefore, chess is deemed more pleasurable.

3) **Certainty:** With chess, assuming you are playing against an opponent of similar skill, there is approximitly a 50% chance of winning and/or losing, whereas with Russian roulette there is only approximitly a 16.67% chance of losing and an 83.33% chance of winning. Under such considerations we can safely surmise that because Russian roulette has better odds of winning versus chess that Russian roulette will be more certainly pleasurable, and the other to be more certainly painful. Yet there's more to consider: when playing any game, winning is not the only source of pleasure; indeed, often the mere thrill of the game and the ensuing camaraderie with your fellow players is enough to make the notion of winning or losing to be but a side note. Add to this the fact of Russian roulette's possibility of ending in death, this "side note" becomes imbued with far more meaning and repercussions. As such, I argue that this tips the scale in favor of chess being more certain to be pleasurable and Russian roulette being more certain to be painful. However, by combining the former Certainty consideration with the latter, we arrive at a Certainty stalemate. Therefore we

need not consider the games' Certainty in our hedonic calculus.

4) Propinquity: The nearness of the pleasure for both games will differ depending on the circumstance, so in this category we can consider it a tie between both games.

5) Fecundity: The probability of further pleasure is in favor of chess, for it is not likely that continued play of Russian roulette will lead to further pleasure, but rather instead death. Therefore by this criteria chess will lead to greater pleasure.

6) Purity: The probability of further pain is in favor of Russian roulette, as outlined in the discussion on fecundity. Therefore by this measure chess will lead to greater pleasure.

7) Extant: Whereas chess is a game between only two individuals, Russian roulette can theoretically be played by any number of individuals, making Russian roulette the favorable choice when seeking pleasure as per this criterion.

By keeping score simply, giving 1 hedon to either chess or Russian roulette for every measure outlined, we find that chess has 3 hedons, while Russian roulette has 2 hedons. Therefore, by using Bentham's criteria we have discovered that playing chess is more likely to lead to happiness rather than playing Russian roulette.

To be charitable to Bentham's theory it must be added that we can further complicate the calculus by factoring in the dolors won by each measure, and yet still further add to the equation a spectrum of hedons and dolors — say on a scale of 1 to 10, with 10 being the highest amount of pleasure or pain and 1 being the lowest. But this poses a problem: Holding pleasure to be a singular sensation along a spectrum leaves us wondering what constitutes the base hedonic value. Won't this value vary depending on the individual?

JOHN STUART MILL

The nineteenth century British philosopher John Stuart Mill solves this problem with his emphasis on a spectrum of felt sensations that vary in quality.

According to Mill, pleasures of low quality (such as eating a cookie or taking a nap) do not have as much an affect on us as higher quality pleasures (such as reading poetry or studying philosophy). The philosopher defined these higher quality pleasures as whatever involves the human capacity for reason and appreciation of aesthetic beauty. This explains his famous saying:

> "*It is far better to be Socrates dissatisfied than a pig satisfied.*"[8]

Meaning, if given the choice, people will always choose the higher qualities of human rationality even if otherwise unsatisfied, rather than the life of a pig, whose only capable of low quality pleasures

---

[8]Mill, John Stuart. *Utilitarianism*. 1863

even if completely satisfied. Humans are rational creatures, authors of their own existence, and this rationality should be celebrated for it leads to high quality human happiness. In this way Mill is like Epicurus, in that he advocates for high quality pleasures, however Mill's pleasures don't quite reach Epicurus' standards.

This theory has its own problem, however. Consider prisoners of the Nazi concentration camps. They may have had the gift of human reason, yet despite the presence of such a high quality pleasure they lacked even the base pleasures of adequate food and shelter. It cannot be asserted that these individuals were happy, but according to Mill's theory it can be argued that should be regarded as happy.

To unpack a better defense for hedonism, let's turn to Chapter Three.

CHAPTER THREE

ATTITUDINAL HEDONISM

Are You Happy With The State Of Affairs?

"What transpires in the mind is just as real as any flesh and blood occurrence."

— Richard Matheson

ATTITUDINAL HEDONISM

DANIEL KAHNEMAM

*I*n the previous chapter we discussed two forms of hedonism. We'll continue that discussion by exploring a third strand of hedonism espoused by the psychologist Daniel Kahneman, a theory known as modified quantitative hedonism. His theory states that what contributes to happiness varies from moment to moment, regardless of our past experiences and regardless of reality. To support his claim, the psychologist notes a discrepancy in the role of life circumstances to our happiness, believing that our individual life circumstances have a smaller role in our happiness than our inherited temperament and personality. [9] He concludes that (1) no matter what happens to us we will all get along one way or another until we die, and (2) some people have a natural tendency towards positivity or negativity.

Kahneman believes that people with a natural tendency for positivity have a "happiness resilience" that brings them back to a "sense of normalcy" even after distressing circumstances. Kahneman refers to this as the "treadmill effect:" the notion that though individuals may experience emotionally

---

[9] Mulnix, Jennifer Wilson; Mulnix, M.J. *Theories of Happiness: An Anthology*. Broadview Press, 2015 — p. 36

intense reactions to life circumstances that have a major impact on their lives, "these reactions appear to subside more or less completely and often quickly."[10] Consider the example of what happens when we swim in a cool pool of water. At first the temperature comes as a cold shock to the body, yet over a relatively short period of time the body gradually adapts to the water.

With this in mind, Kahneman suggests there exists a "satisfaction treadmill," which promotes happiness as a scale of achievement "that lies somewhere between realistic expectation and reasonable hope" noting that "people are always satisfied when they attain their aspiration level."[11]

FOCUS

When I was young boy I used to shoot archery with my brother and my father. We would shoot compound bow, which is different from the more traditional bow in that it use cables and pulleys to help pull the limbs of the bow back with far greater ease. It also have what's called "sights," which are little pins that help you set up your aim. Depending on far away you estimate your target is — whether 100 yards, 200 yards, or so forth — you line up the appropriate sight on your bow with your target. These sights set you to aim higher or lower

---

[10] Ibid. — p. 36
[11] Ibid. — p. 37

depending on the distance. If your target is close, you aim low; if it is farther away, the sights help you aim higher.

The idea is that if you have a good bow made of strong materials, and if your distance estimate is accurate, and if your aim is good — if line up your sights just right and if you release with confidence — then the arrow has no choice but to hit its target.

I was fairly young when we would go to the archery "shoots" as they're called, yet even though I was so young I received several trophies for my archery accomplishments. To be clear, it had nothing to do with my ability; rather, I was one of the only kids in my age bracket! It's easy to be number one if you're the only one!

The point is this: There are many reasons why an arrow might miss its mark: Maybe the bow was defective, or maybe the distance estimate was wrong, or perhaps the release was shaky so the arrow flew off course. There are many reasons why an arrow might miss its mark, but one thing is positively certain to cause an arrow to miss, and that's by focusing on the wrong things.

THE PITTSBURGH STORY

Back in early February of 2007 I was on tour with a band. I was their opening act doing my magic show. The band was an experimental electronica trio called *The Ear, The Eye, and The Arm*. I liked to think of myself as the "leg" during that tour, because even though they were only a trio, they had a lot of equipment, so I would help with the legwork of carrying their speakers, amplifiers, instruments, and various boxes of miscellaneous cables, from the tour van and into the whatever club we were performing in that day.

We started off in Massachusetts, made it as far south as Washington DC, and then made it as far north as Burlington, VT.   On our way through Pennsylvania we stopped for a show in Pittsburgh. On this particular evening, in February of 2007 in Pittsburgh, PA, we had just finished unloading all of the band's equipment, and then I went back out to the street to get my suitcase out of the van so I could start preparing for my set. As I was approaching the van I became abundantly aware of two street thugs lurking nearby. And I knew they were street thugs, because I've watched television, and these guys were classic street thugs. Have any of you met a real, live, street thug before?

My natural reaction was to go back to the club and wait for the thugs to scamper off — or whatever it is that thugs do — but then I hesitated. I hesitated because I thought to myself: *"I don't actually know that these guys are street thugs. That's just my assumptions. That's just society, and the media, and my fears, all making me jump to conclusions about a couple of people that I truly know nothing about."* So I ignored my fears and went to the van.

Just as I got to the sliding door of the van I felt two strong arms push me up against the van and the street thugs proceeded to mug me. Yes, it turns out my fear were well founded. Now, I had never been mugged before, so this was all very new and exciting! And it all happened quite quickly so before I knew it they were scampering off with my wallet (yes, it turns out that street thugs do indeed scamper). I was still probably in a bit of shock as I finally pulled my suitcase from the van and went inside just in time to start my set!

When I got to the stage, I began by saying: *"So I was just mugged outside..."* — and everyone thought it was part of my act. They thought it was a joke! I told them: *"No, I'm serious! It's terrible to be here! I don't want to be in Pittsburgh anymore — I want go home!"*

Again, the mugging happened so quickly that it took me a while to fully process what had happened, but when I did I realized something quite profound, and this is really what I wanted to share with you folks. The muggers were actually rather nice. ... I know that might sound strange, but it's true! It was all in their words! This is what they said, after pushing me up against the van, they said: *"Stay cool! Give it up!"*

Do you see what I mean? In order to "stay cool" you have to originally "be cool." They were complimenting me! They thought I was a pretty cool guy! It was by far the most positive mugging experience I had ever had. It was also the only mugging experience I've ever had. ... Again, it all happened very quickly so I didn't get a chance to process that at the time, because if I had I would have offered them a tip. I mean, they took all my money wallet and all anyway, but I could have at least offered them my pin number.

Regardless, the whole point of this story is to show you the silver lining, which is this: I now know the true meaning of the named Pittsburgh "Stealers."

FOCUS ON THE POSITIVE

I tell you that story, partially for the ridiculous pun, but also to highlight my main objective for being with you today.

I used to tell that mugging story as part of another presentation, and one day someone came up to me afterwards and told me that he loved the Pittsburgh story. So asked him what it was about that story that resonated with him. He told me that had this same experience happened to him he would not have been able to find a way to laugh at it.

Until that moment I wasn't really aware on a conscious level that my way of thinking was anything special or different. But what this person told me, changed my perspective and got me to reflect. Take two people and put them into the same situation. One person can came away from it feeling bitter, and yet another person walk away from the same experience fascinated by the whole thing!

What I'm suggesting is that regardless of the circumstances or the criticism that we may encounter, that we find a way to focus on the positive. It's kind of like the age-old saying: when life gives is lemons, what do we do? Get a new life? No! We make lemonade.

A MAGIC RIDDLE

Let's unpack this a bit more by testing your imagination with a little magic trick and a riddle:

> *Imagine that there are three white plastic cups sitting face down on a table. There is also a little red ball that is hiding in my right pocket.*

> *I'm going to sneak the ball out of my pocket and place it secretly underneath one of the cups, and you're not going to see me do it — because I'm an awesome magician with incredible sleight of hand, of course.*

> *Your job is to try and guess which cup the ball is under but, here's the thing, you can only choose One.*

> *Do you think the ball underneath cup number One, Cup Number Two, or Cup Number Three?*

So, what cup is the ball under?

...and The Pursuit of Happiness

Have you guessed?

If you thought that the ball is underneath Cup Number One then you are correct Congratulations! You get the High Five Award!

I suppose you might be wondering why the ball is underneath Cup Number One. It is quite simple: I told you that you could *"only choose One."*

The words matter, and not just when you're being mugged in Pittsburgh!

KEEP FOCUSING

We all have our own examples from our own lives of how easy it is to get distracted. We focus on the wrong things, and miss the important things that are right in front of us. We get distracted by the responsibilities of everyday life and for too many days, or weeks, or months in a row, we kind of fall asleep, or get hypnotized by the repetitive cycles we find ourselves in.

It's like what sometimes happens when we're driving a car: we get lost in thought and all of a sudden we've arrived at our destination but with no recollection of the various twists and turns that got us there. Sometimes we have entire days, and weeks, and months like this. I know people who have gone entire years where they're stuck in the cycle of doing things and going places, going to work , going through the motions of getting things done, but they're not consciously aware of what or why we are doing these things.

Have you ever experienced this? Perhaps you're experiencing this right now! Perhaps you're asking yourself, *"How did I get here?"*

REFLECTIONS

1) *How have you been feeling lately?*

2) *How have you been feeling about your work?*

3) *How have you been feeling about your family, your relationship with them, and the direction you're all going?*

4) *How have you been feeling about yourself?*

And as a follow-up question: are you getting the results in any or all of these areas that you're looking for? If so, high five! Nice job! Now don't lose focus. Reflect on how you can aim even higher.

But if you're not getting the results that you want, then take a look at your focus. Take a look at what you've been giving your attention to.

- *Take a look at your calendar, your daily agenda: where do you focus your time?*
- *Take a look at your bank account: where do you focus your money?*

When I'm missing the mark for too long, those are often the first places that I'll find that a refocus is needed.

By proactively asking these kinds of questions, everyday, and actually doing the work to make positive changes, it will help us be more awake, be more aware, be more focused, and actively engaged in our daily lives.

FRED FELDMAN

If we are attracted to this idea of a happiness treadmill, and like the idea that carefully directing our focus to achieve happiness, then perhaps we'll like this thing called attitudinal hedonism, as espoused by the contemporary American professor of philosophy at the University of Massachusetts, Fred Feldman, who believes that happiness is *"a positive psychological stance toward some object, which may or may not be accompanied by any felt quality."*[12] According to Feldman, happiness is understood as taking pleasure in the "states of affairs."[13] In this way, something may not necessarily "feel" good, but we may still be pleased by the "state of affairs."

Feldman offers two hypothetical examples to support this theory, of which I will offer a slightly modified version:

(1) Dolores experiences debilitating pain on a regular basis but takes a pain management drug alleviating her pain to a certain degree. Though still in severe pain, Dolores' pain has subsided

---

[12] Mulnix, Jennifer Wilson; Mulnix, M.J. *Happy Lives, Good Lives: A Philosophical Examination.* Broadview Press, 2015 — p. 62

[13] Mulnix, Jennifer Wilson; Mulnix, M.J. *Theories of Happiness: An Anthology.* Broadview Press, 2015 — p. 65

significantly and, according to Feldman, this makes her happy due to the "state of affairs."

(2) Wendell purchases a massage chair that promises to give the greatest massage you can ever imagine. With expectations high, Wendell was disappointed to find that it produced only a mildly pleasing massage. Even while feeling pleasure, Feldman asserts that it cannot be argued that Wendell is happy, because they experience did not meet his expectation.[14] He was not happy with the state of affairs.

These examples aside, one problem with Feldman's theory is that it doesn't rely on truth. He argues that *"we can experience pleasure, both in the attitudinal and feeling sense, even when our experiences are illusionary"* [15] because occurrent (or actually occurring) attitudinal pleasures do not rely on truth.[16]

As an example, we can believe something to be true and be comforted by it, but this thing we believe can actually be entirely false. The *experience* of a good lie can positively affect attitudinal pleasure. We may take comfort in believing that we have a loving and faithful spouse, even if the truth

---

[14] Ibid. — p. 62

[15] Mulnix, Jennifer Wilson; Mulnix, M.J. *Happy Lives, Good Lives: A Philosophical Examination.* Broadview Press, 2015 — p. 98

[16] Mulnix, Jennifer Wilson; Mulnix, M.J. *Theories of Happiness: An Anthology.* Broadview Press, 2015 — p. 70

of the matter is that the spouse constantly cheats on us. The theory being, "what we don't know won't hurt us."

DANIEL HAYBRON

If we have trouble supporting a theory of happiness that doesn't rely on truth then perhaps we can look to the St. Louis University Philosopher, Daniel Haybron, who believes that the true source of an individual's happiness is their "emotional state."[17] If one is happy it's because they have a predominance of "joyfulness, high-spiritedness, peace of mind," and the like. Happiness therefore is understood as a "dispositional phenomenon" that reflects an individual's history and potential for future tendencies. But how does one develop such a positive state of mind?

RETHINKING POSITIVE THINKING

There's some misunderstanding about what it really means to be positive. A lot of people think that it's about wearing rose-colored glasses, walking around ignoring reality and believing that everything is fine and dandy even when it isn't. Even when we're clearly in a bad situation yet forge ahead anyway. That's not positivity; that's ridiculous!

---

[17] Ibid. — p. 100

36

THE ACID ROULETTE STORY

When I was fourteen years old I was invited to perform my magic act at my high school talent show. I decided that I wanted to an exciting, impressive magic trick in the show ... and what's more exciting than something death-defying? So I spent some time thinking about it came up with the perfect demonstration: Russian roulette!

Of course, I was just fourteen years old and this was going to be at my high school, so I couldn't use a revolver. Instead, I used five test tubes, and each test tube was filled with water except for one which contained hydrochloric acid! Hydrochloric acid is colorless, it's odorless; it looks and smells just like water...but it certainly doesn't taste like water! The idea was that I would be blindfolded, and the test tubes would be mixed up, rearranged on the table by a member of the audience. My job was to avoid the test tube with the acid, and drink the contents of the other four test tubes, without drinking the acid. That was the idea.

On the night of the talent show, I was blindfolded, the test tubes were mixed up, I stepped behind the table, picked up the one of the test tubes, and drank it — and then I immediately spit it out, tore off the blindfold, and ran off the stage, because I had just drank the acid! And everyone thought it was part of the act! They just laughed and laughed! I was wearing a wireless microphone so everyone could hear me yelling for help, and asking for my mother ... who also happened to be in the audience. She was freaking out!

On our way to the hospital I was hanging out of the car window spitting, because the acid had eaten away at my esophagus so I couldn't swallow. And despite this scary moment in my life, I still had the presence of mind in that moment, to turn to my mother and say: *"We must never speak of this!"*

I ended up in the hospital on a feeding tube, because I couldn't eat solid food ... which was just as well, because the acid also ate away my taste buds, so I couldn't taste anything anyway. But there is good news, I found out something fascinating: that acid whitens your teeth. And that's how I stumbled across the secret to a great smile!

I tell you this story, because I was "positive" that I was going to be able to successfully perform that trick that night, because I had practiced it! Of course I didn't use acid in rehearsal — why practice something that you can only fail once? So in rehearsal, instead of acid, I used seltzer, and it worked fine, most of the time. Sometimes I drank the seltzer by mistake. But as the performance approached I put on a "positive attitude" about the whole thing, but this attitude ignored the reality of my circumstances. I was ignoring the fact that this was probably not a good idea! That's not positivity — that's ridiculous!

DEVELOP CONFIDENCE

When I suggest that we focus on the positive I'm not referring to attitude; rather, I'm referring to confidence. Think about it: when we say that we're positive of something, do we mean that we're not too sure? Do we mean that we only think something is true? Or do we mean that we are confident of it? I suggest that when we say that we are positive we mean that we are confident because we are sure, and we are sure because we know the truth, and we know the truth because we have taken in an honest assessment of reality.

And this brings us to a key point on our pursuit: positivity requires an honest assessment of our circumstances, but we get to choose the frame we use to display our circumstances to ourselves and those around us. This frame is made of the words that we focus on, and these words can either lift us up, or drag us down.

In any given situation there's at least two ways that we perceive what's happening:

1) With negativity and suspicion, or
2) With positivity and excitement.

We can choose to see the world as something out there to get us, or we can choose to see the world as an opportunity to grow regardless of circumstances. As leadership expert John Maxwell puts it:

"Sometimes you win, sometimes you learn!"[18]

The good news is that we have that choice, and it all depends on what we choose to feed.

THE TWO WOLVES

I'm reminded of the Cherokee legend of the two wolves:

> *A fight is going on inside me. A terrible fight between two wolves.*
>
> *One is evil: doubt, anger, envy, sorrow, regret, greed, arrogance, self-pity, guilt, resentment, lies, ego.*
>
> *The other is good: confidence, peace, love, joy, serenity, humility, kindness, empathy, generosity, truth, compassion, faith.*
>
> *The same fight is going on inside you and inside every other person, too.*
>
> *Which wolf will win? The one you feed.*

We can choose the frame we use to display our circumstances. This frame is made of words that we focus on, and these words can either lift us up, or drag us down. Choosing to feed the good wolf helps us develop confidence to always be happy with the state of our affairs.

FRAMING WITH POSITIVITY

---

[18] Maxwell, John. *Sometimes You Win, Sometimes You Learn.* Center Street, 2012

40

Think of an experience you've had that you remember as being negative. Perhaps it's an experience from long ago; maybe it happened more recently; or maybe it's something that you're going through right now. Think about the circumstances. Think about the people involved. Think about the feelings that it invokes. Think about the words that you use to describe this situation. Doubt, anger, envy, sorrow, regret, greed, arrogance, self-pity, guilt, resentment, lies, ego. What words would you use to describe this situation? We're going to remove these words from our box. We're not ignoring the reality of the situation, but we are choosing to honor it with the benefit of positivity. Choose new words: confidence, peace, love, joy, serenity, humility, kindness, empathy, generosity, truth, compassion, faith. Sit with your situation redefined, reframed with these positive words. Sit with this feeling. Take a deep breath in, let it out.

CHANGE THE SHAPE OF AN ICECUBE

We have the ability to choose the frame we use to display our circumstances. This frame is made of the words that we focus on, and these words can either lift us up, or drag us down.

If this way of thinking doesn't come naturally then we can think of it as changing the shape of an ice cube: melt it down, decide the new shape, and then refreeze the water in that new shape.

Changing the way we see your circumstances is the same process. I'm reminded of the words that the Pittsburgh street thugs used: "Stay cool; give it up." We have to "give up" our old way of seeing things, allow it to melt away, so that we can choose a new more positive way of thinking, and then practice this new way of thinking everyday, and follow through with it until it freezes into a habit.

The is not an easy process but the important thing to remember is to just start: start where you are, start with just one thing, and start with making small changes.

But maybe happiness truly has nothing to do with pleasure. But if not, then what might it entail? Let's turn to Chapter Four to explore our options.

CHAPTER FOUR

EUDEMONISM

Realize Your Full Human Potential!

"Carpe diem. Seize the day, boys. Make your lives extraordinary."

— John Keating

EUDEMONISM

So far in our pursuit of happiness we've explored the various ways that pleasure contributes to happiness from the hedonic perspective. In this chapter we'll explore a different approach beyond pleasure.

ROBERT NOZICK

Robert Nozick is a Harvard professor of philosophy who believes that there exist things outside of pleasure that contribute to our happiness. To prove this he created a thought experiment famously known as "The Experience Machine."

Imagine a machine that you can be hooked up to that will give you any experiential sensation you can think of. The machine would be so well-made that there would be no way for you to know whether you are already hooked up to the machine or not, because once in the machine you would forget that you had premeditated all of the experiences programmed into the machine. This machine will give you all the wonderful experiences that you've always wanted, with only the good feelings and no pesky negative feelings. The only difference is that these feelings would only be sensational; the things you'd be experiencing wouldn't actually be happening. The point of this thought experiment is that you must decide if you would agree to enter this machine for the rest of your natural life.

Nozick believes that this thought experiment proves that happiness cannot be reduced to feelings alone, because he believes that few would agree to use such a machine. Your own answer to this thought experiment indicates an evaluation of what you deem most appropriate for obtaining the best possible life for yourself.[19] If you would enter the machine then you are a hedonist; if you would not enter the machine then you are something else, and it this "something" else that we will explore in the ensuing chapters

ARISTOTLE

To avoid holding ourselves we can look to the ancient Greek philosopher Aristotle who has a theory of happiness that states *"living well and doing well are the same as being happy."*[20] Happiness of this kind is termed eudemonia, which refers to living "an excellent human life," fulfilling one's fullest potential in all areas of virtue. In short, happiness means to flourish. Aristotle believed that to be happy was to achieve the highest attainment of virtues, such as honor, courage, temperance, understanding, truthfulness, modesty, and so forth.

---

[19] Mulnix, Jennifer Wilson; Mulnix, M.J. *Theories of Happiness: An Anthology*. Broadview Press, 2015 — p. 250
[20] Ibid. — p. 323

The key for understanding Aristotle's theory, however, is seeing it as a constant striving for virtuous greatness; a process rather than a destination. It is a continuous activity, just as *"one swallow does not make a spring, nor...does one day or a short time make us blessed and happy."*[21] To grow in virtue and therefore increase our chance for happiness, we focus on developing good habits to fully express what we our capable of. For this reason it is said: *"We become just by doing just actions, temperate by doing temperate actions, brave by doing brave actions"*[22] We become happy by facing difficult situations and responding in a virtuously, even if we lack the mastery. Our muscles grow by adding resistance, not by avoiding resistance.

ENEMY OF THE GOOD

Not long after graduating high school I went to New York City with some fellow magicians. We went to see a show called Monday Night Magic, a weekly magic show that features different magicians every week. I had never been to the show before so I was excited to see what it was all about. There was this one particular magician there that night named Levent, and he was incredible! This guy was a double threat: not only was he technically flawless in his sleight of hand, but he was also hilarious! By

---

[21] Aristotle. The Nicomachean Ethics
[22] Ibid.

the time Levent's act was over my stomach was in pain from laughing so hard, and my face hurt from smiling so much.

One of the friends I was with was an older gentleman, he was kind of a "magic mentor" to me, and seeing how completely and thoroughly entertained I was by Levent, and also knowing of own my aspirations for growing as a performer, he pulled me aside after the show and told me:

"Don't let the great be the enemy of the good."

What he meant was that just because someone somewhere is better than you at something that doesn't mean it's any less of a worthy endeavor for you. This advice is a fantastic motivator to get us into the game, but it does have a dark side.

THE DANGERS OF "GOOD ENOUGH"

After spending years invested in this philosophy, I realized that I had taken the idea too far. I realized that I had become content with being a "good enough" and was never interested in even *trying* to improve. I realized that I wasn't in the game to win; I was in the game to not lose.

Do you see the difference? I didn't want to experience the pain of failure, or rejection, because I figured I wasn't all that great anyway, so I held back and played life small. One of my colleagues used to often tell me to *"go large or go home!"* And you know what I'd say? I'd say, *"I'm just gonna to go home!"* I wasn't in it to win it. The same philosophy that got me into the game was now keeping me from growing. Over time I came to understand a new mantra: *"Don't let your own good work become the stumbling stone that keeps you from becoming your very best."* Because doing only what is expected of us is good enough; but our very best is always found in doing more than expected. It's found in going the extra mile. "Good enough" is not good enough when we're capable of so much more!

PULLING BACK THE REIGHS

Have you ever ridden a horse? I never have, but I have ridden a pony. Fun fact about ponies: did you know that ponies can't talk? It's because they're a little horse.

(I'll pause a moment to make sure you had a chance to chuckle.)

The moral of the story is this: it's said that one of the greatest tragedies of life is when we pull back the reins on our horse just before it's about to leap. In other words: don't let your good work became the stumbling stone that keeps you from becoming your very best.

REFLECTIONS

1) *Have you been accepting "good enough" as good enough? If not, then high five! Because you've*

49

> *acknowledge that your work and your life can be so much more than your current level of achievement.*

But if you're answer is yes, that you have been content with "good enough," then my follow question is this:

> 2) *What's holding you back? What gap is preventing you from moving forward? How is it keeping you from achieving more?*

It's said that everything we do or don't do can have catastrophic consequences ... for us, for others, and for our environment. Our goal should not be to merely slide by each day, but rather to be always aware, always looking, to ensure that at the end of the day everyone makes it back home safely. When the stakes are that high, "good enough" can't be good enough.

To help us assess the reality of our circumstances, I compiled a list of common gaps that many people encounter in life. Actually, I didn't compile this list; my mentor John Maxwell did. But I've personally faced a number of these gaps myself, and perhaps you have too. I'll read each one and just listen carefully and think about which gap most closely relates to your situation:

> 1) **The Assumption Gap:** *"I assume that I will automatically grow, develop, and advance in life."*

> 2) **The Knowledge Gap:** *"I don't know how to grow. I don't know what I need to do to better my life."*

3) **The Timing Gap:** *"It's not the right time to begin."*

4) **The Mistake Gap:** *"I'm afraid of making mistakes. I'm afraid to look like a failure."*

5) **The Perfection Gap:** *"I have to find the best way before I start. I have to know all the facts before I begin. I have to already be perfect before I launch."*

6) **The Inspiration Gap:** *"I don't feel like doing it. I'm not in the mood."*

7) **The Comparison Gap:** *"Others are better than I am, so why bother trying?"*

8) **The Expectation Gap:** *"I thought it would be easier than this."*

ENGAGE YOUR GAP

What does your gap look like? Today I suggest that you "Engage Your Gap." What I mean by this, is don't ignore it hoping that it will just go away, but instead engage it, making small incremental changes to get back on track.

NASA reports that when they launch a rocket it's off course 90% of the time! That's almost the *entire* time! So it has to always move forward making small incremental changes, in order to go the distance and reach its target destination. It's only by acknowledging where the rocket is off course — and then making the appropriate changes — that the rocket is able to reach its destination. If it works for NASA, then I suggest that it can also work for us.

TURN "*CAN I?*" INTO "*HOW CAN I?*"

Facing difficult situations makes us stronger if we approach them by expressing our virtuous nature, even if we haven't mastered these virtues yet. And perhaps a good place to start acting this way is by asking a different kind of question. This is what I have in mind: when we get an idea for something that's important to our improvement, instead of asking ourselves "*Can I do this?*" we should instead ask "*How can I do this?*" The two questions sound similar but they have a significant difference:

"*Can I*" contains inherent doubt, imposing a limitation that undermines our efforts before we even begin. This limitation has nothing to do with a lack of ability, but rather a lack of confidence.

By contrast, the question "*How Can I*" presupposes that we *can*, that it *is* possible, that there is a way, and that we just need to find it. This question alone begins to stack the deck in our favor.

SHORT-CIRCUIT YOUR WEAKNESSES

One of my weaknesses is that at the end of the day, I know that when given the option between sleep and exercise, sleep always wins. I short-circuited this weakness, by acknowledging something else about myself: I don't like to bed without first taking a shower. I call it "getting the day off of me." So you know what I did? I moved into an apartment that doesn't have a shower. There isn't even a bathtub where I live. So if I want to go to bed, then I have to take a shower first, but in order to do that I have to drive two towns over to the gym ... and if I'm already at the gym I end up working out! By asking the question *"How Can I?"* I enabled myself to lose over seventy pounds, effectively short-circuiting one of my weaknesses.

DEVELOP CONFIDENCE

Perhaps the best answer to this question of "how" is found in one simple word: confidence.

Earlier we talked about how easy it is to be confident when the deck is stacked in our favor. But what if we don't have that luxury? What if we're not prepared? When that happens we begin a process of losing control of the direction our lives:

We develop an unrealistic perspective of how life works, often asking: *"Why Me?"* And when we ask *"Why Me?"* we develop the victim mindset ... seeing the world, other people, circumstances, policies and procedures, as opposing forces against us. And when we do that, we hand over the responsibility of our success and happiness to others. We give away our ability to control the direction of our lives.

The only solution to change that, is by developing confidence. When we're confident we have a realistic perspective of life and proactively look for ways to grow and improve. When we're confident we see that the world isn't out to get us but rather it's there to conspire with us. And when we're confident we become fully engaged with the direction of our lives.

When I was young I was incredibly shy, would barely even speak to my family, and when I did speak I had a significant, severe, stutter. Even my own parents had a difficult time understanding me when I spoke. What helped me move beyond that struggle was learning magic. From an early age I discovered that I had a natural talent for it, but in order to perform magic I had to get in front of others and speak. I was able to confidently step forward and perform because I knew I had something wonderful to share, which gave me the confidence to step forward.

What this suggests is that our confidence is found by capitalizing on our strengths, on what we do well. Your very best will always be found in doing what you already do well, in what you are already talented in. Even Aristotle admitted that it is rare to find a truly happy person, because those who are strong in certain virtues are weak in others. I suggest that if we like this eudemonistic theory of happiness, then capitalizing on your natural strengths can help you develop the confidence you need to successfully short circuit your weaknesses and achieve happiness.

In this way, short-circuiting your weakness and capitalizing on your strength is a magic formula for developing confidence.

REFLECTIONS

1) *What do you need to do to short-circuit your weaknesses?*

2) *What do you need to do to capitalize on your strengths.*

3) *How would your life be better if you "stacked your deck" to be more confident?*

DEVELOP BETTER HABITS

For everything we gain, we give something up. If we want to improve our life then we have to sacrifice something else.

A friend of mine often tells me:

"When you're walking towards something you're also walking away from something." [23]

So as you consider ways of "stacking your deck" consider too what you are willing to walk away from so that you can achieve more than you're currently experiencing?

We will never change our lives until we change something that we do daily. Ultimately people don't decide their future; rather, people decide on what they do day-to-day — they decide on their habits — and it's their habits that decide their future.

---

[23] Thank you, Jimmy Ridlin!

Pursuing happiness by living a life of "eudemonia" calls us to live an excellent human life by developing and fostering virtuous habits. If this view of happiness appeals to you then this just might be the path to happiness for you.

CHAPTER FIVE

LIFE SATISFACTIONISM

A Roadmap For Living Your Dream

"You'll have bad times, but it'll always wake you up to the good stuff you weren't paying attention to."

— Sean Maguire

LIFE SATISFACTIONISM

RICHARD KRAUT

*N*orthwestern University professor of philosophy Richard Kraut takes a subjective approach to happiness that believes the happy person is the one who meets their own self-imposed standards of living, finds their life to be desirable, and that nothing more could be done to improve their life.[24]

In this view, happiness is created by an individual imposing personal standards of living and creating goals in order to live the life that they believe would lead to the cultivation of the best version of themselves.[25] Merely being in a positive psychological state does not make a eudemon life, rather seeking to *actually* live a eudemon life instigates the psychological state that indicates a positive self-assessment.

This flexible subjective approach to happiness allows us to choose our own path in the pursuit of happiness, and I would suggest that it also indicates the radical notion that happiness can be achieved even when unfortunate life circumstances intervene.

DANGEROUS GAMES

---

[24] Mulnix, Jennifer Wilson; Mulnix, M.J. *Theories of Happiness: An Anthology*. Broadview Press, 2015 — p. 372
[25] Ibid. — p. 363

The comedian Steven Wright, puts it well when he says:

"Sometimes even when you lose you win; like playing musical electric chairs."[26]

That's a game we don't want to win. Heck, that's a game we shouldn't even be playing! What this suggests, then, is that the next time we find ourselves in a losing situation we should try to look at it from another perspective. If we do we may find that what we've been after is not really in your best interest after all. We may discover that the game we've been playing is really a game of musical electric chairs.

By holding a life satisfactionism view of happiness we are able to achieve happiness even in so-called "losing situations" because we no longer view such circumstances as failure, but rather as signposts guiding us through the maze of life.

I'm reminded of the story of two men convicted of a crime and as punishment sentenced to walking across a tight rope over a deep chasm. The first man quickly walked to the other side, and the second man yelled across the way for advice. To this the man replied:

---

[26] Wright, Steven. *When The Leave Blow Away*. 2007

"How should I know? All I did was this. When I found myself listing to one side, I leaned to the other."[27]

NAPOLEON HILL

The author Napoleon Hill puts it another way when he says that the worst things that can happen to you could be the best thing that could happen to you, so long as you don't let it get the best of you.[28] This positive mental attitude approach is admittedly easier said than done, I know from personal experience; but I also know from personal experience that when you work everyday to foster that perspective, it will reveal a whole other world to you. It will reveal hidden meanings in the events around you.

THE CHOKING WOMAN

In the summer of 2007 I was working at a restaurant in East Windsor Connecticut, La Notte Restaurant. I was the house magician and my job was to perform close-up magic for people, distracting then from the fact that their food still hadn't arrived. One night I was performing in the dinning room and there was a commotion across the room. There was a crowd of people around an elderly couple, maybe in the early to mid eighties, and I realized out that the woman had choked on a piece of food.

---

[27] de Mello, Anthony. *Taking Flight*. Doubleday, 1988.
[28] Hill, Napoleon. *Napoleon Hill's Keys to Success: The 17 Principles of Personal Achievement*. Penguin, 1997.

She was okay but quite distraught. I went over to distract her. I didn't perform any magic for her, but she shared with me her story:

Just a few weeks earlier she had eaten at the same restaurant, sat at the same table, and also choked on her food. I stopped her there and told her that if she wants to eat here that she should probably sit at a different table. (She ignored my attempt at humor and continued her story.)

On that day it was different. She couldn't cough up her food, and a man from the bar had to come over and perform the Heimlich maneuverer on her. He pounded and pounded on this frail old woman for what must have seemed like an eternity. Her husband told me that at one point her face started to turn grey ... she as on her way out, when finally she was able to cough up her food and breath.

By this time the paramedics had arrived and even though she was breathing fine they brought her to the hospital as a precaution, fearing that her ribs may have been broken from the pounding she had just received. When she arrived at the hospital the doctors didn't find any broken ribs ... but they did find an aneurism that was about to burst.

This was someone's grandmother ... someone's mother. Had this near death experience not happened she surely would have died. This eighty-something year old woman had lived her entire life, yet it was not her time to go. Yet there could be a young woman, no more twenty-six years old, and it could just be her time to leave.

It can be said that there's nothing good about tragedy, that it is better to be happy than sad and better to be at peace than in chaos; yet just as choking on a piece of food can have a greater meaning, so too can tragedy, sadness, and chaos have a deeper meaning, if you're open to looking at it from a different perspective.

REFLECTIONS

1) *What are you choking on?*

2) *Are you playing a game you shouldn't be playing?*

3) *Should you be leaning in another direction?*

DREAM VISUALIZATION

Think back to when you were a little child. Maybe to when you were 5, 6, 7, or 8 years old. Think about what you wanted to be when you grow. What was your childhood dream. It very well could be the path that you're currently on, or it could be a long forgotten dream, a dream that you passed on for something else as your circumstances changed. Whatever the case may be, hold that dream in mind for a moment. Take a deep breath in, and take a deep breath out.

PURPOSE

As children we're often told what we can't do. *"You can't do this, you can't do that; sit down, shut up."* But with magic even the impossible is possible. When I was a young boy I saw the magician David Copperfield fly through the air like a bird! He made the Statue of Liberty Disappear! He walked through the Great Wall of China! This man was breaking all the rules, because he wasn't just doing what he wasn't *supposed* to do — he was doing what no one is supposed to be *able* to do!

That's how I knew even from a young age that I wanted to be a magician. In support of my ambition my mother made a cape for me and my father gave me a gentleman's top hat. I'd go out into the yard and find sticks and run around the neighborhood yelling *"ABRACADABRA!"* My neighbors thought I was crazy — which was probably true — but I had the last laugh when one day the person I was pretending to be became the person that I am, because on that day I became a magician.

It was June 12, 1996, at Warren Community Elementary, I was just 12 years old, and it was there that I became a magician by performing my very first magic show.

I tell you this story, and I encouraged you to reflect on your own dreams, to highlight an important step in creating self-imposed standards of living, which is to define your purpose. To understand the importance of this it's important to understand a common mistake that many people make when defining their purpose: It's when we confuse who we are with what we do.

The author Neale Donald Walsch points out:

"We are human beings, not human doings."

This suggests that we have two purposes: an inner purpose, which concerns *being*; and an outer purpose, which concerns *doing*.

When you consider your inner purpose you ask questions like:

1) *Who do you want to be? What kind of person do you want to be?*

2) *What are your values (meaning literally, what do you value?)*

3) *How will those values inform the way that you will live your life?*

It's by asking these qualifying questions that you gain insight into your outer purpose:

1) *What are your natural talents and abilities?*

2) *What interests fire you up?*

3) *What makes you come alive?*

You will know that you've discovered your outer purpose when your answer to these questions dance in harmony with your values, when what you do is a clear reflection of who you are.

VALARIE TIBERIUS & ALICIA HALL

This investigation of values is what can perhaps bridge the gap between objective and subjective theories of happiness. Valarie Tiberius and Alicia Hall are philosophy professors who teach that the problem with objective theories is that it's difficult to come up with umbrella rules that cover everyone, but also difficult to allow certain activities to be counted as actually leading towards a good life. To overcome these problems this pair of philosophers created what's known as a value-based life satisfaction theory of happiness.[29]

To explain this theory they use the example of a person who likes to eat bagels for breakfast and who also experiences constant intestinal pains. They argue that the desire for bagels will diminish when they find out that their horrific pains are caused by a gluten allergy. They argue that by putting their values in order, valuing sound health over their value for eating bagels, they will become more satisfied with life. Therefore, this theory of happiness prescribes ordering your values, and living according to those values. They say that "Your life goes well for you if you have a good sense of what matters in life and you feel good about your life because you are achieving it."[30]

---

[29] Mulnix, Jennifer Wilson; Mulnix, M.J. *Theories of Happiness: An Anthology*. Broadview Press, 2015 — p. 138
[30] Ibid. — p. 141

ECKHART TOLLE

Tiberius and Hall argue that happiness is equal to satisfaction with life. The obstacle we encounter here is that once we know our values, and once we recognize our strengths and talents and passions, how do we know for what path to take? There's more than one way to achieve anything, so how do we choose our path to happiness?

To answer this question we turn to the German author Eckhart Tolle for what he refers to as "modalities of awakened doing."[31] I use this as a checklist for determining if I'm on the right track, and maybe you'll find it useful to in your own pursuit. In all that you do, do it with Enthusiasm, Enjoyment, and Acceptance.

If you are on the right track living your purpose then it's easy to do everything with enthusiasm. After all, you're on the path to living your dream! Even if you're doing a tedious task   like applying for a job, or filling out college applications, you can do these with enthusiasm!

Okay, maybe you can't do those things with enthusiasm, but you can enjoy the process, knowing that it's going to get you to where you want to be. You can enjoy the process even when you run into

---

[31] Tolle, Eckhart. *A New Earth: Awakening to Your Life's Purpose*. Penguin, 2005.

obstacles that get in your way, like when midterms and finals come around!

Okay, maybe you can't enjoy that, but you can at the very least accept it as a necessary step to achieving your dream.

You will know that you're on the right track when you can do everything with genuine enthusiasm, enjoyment, and acceptance. In a similar way, you will know that you have gone the wrong way if for too many days, or weeks, or months in a row, you can't even accept what you're doing. Perhaps you've been lying to yourself. Maybe you've accepted someone else's dream. Or maybe you're afraid to try, or just don't know what it is you want. Whatever the case may be, if you don't have enthusiasm, enjoyment, and acceptance in your life, then it's a clear sign that it's time to find another way.

REFLECTIONS

1) *What aren't you doing today, because you're afraid to try?*

2) *What aren't you doing today, because you gave up on your dream?*

3) *What aren't you doing today, because you've never had a worthy guide to show you the way?*

PERSISTENCE

Returning to the philosopher that started this discussion, Kraut's idea that happiness is possible even when unfortunate life circumstances intervene is a call to action that requires brave persistence. I can say with confidence that today I am very happy, even though I've had my share of pains and unfortunate circumstances.

My troubles began in 1998 when I met Stephanie. And isn't that way it always is? The downfall of every man and woman is love? Because of I knew it was love — I was just sixteen years old and had never felt that way before, what else could it be!?

One day I mustered the nerve to ask her to go with me to the Winter Semi-Formal. And she said yes! I was so excited when the big day came around: It was Friday December 3, 1999, and at one point, early on in the evening, we were sitting in the chairs along the wall of the darkened cafeteria.

And while we were sitting the first slow song of the night came on. I desperately wanted to dance this song with Stephanie, but I hesitated ... It was a big deal that I even had the nerve to ask her to be my date ... how was I going to get the nerve to ask her to dance with me ... to the *slow* song?!

So there we sat, me trying to muster the nerve to ask her to dance, and her waiting for me to ask. When all of a sudden, out of nowhere, comes this other guy and asks Stephanie for a dance ... who does this guy think he is?! ... And she said yes!

So there I sat on the sidelines, watching everyone else dance. And when the song was over, Stephanie came up to me and, I'll always remember what she said, she said: "You know, Jonas, If you want to dance with me all you have to do is ask."

It was maybe a week or two after that that I mustered the nerve to tell Stephanie exactly how I felt about her. And you know what she said to me? She said, "Jonas, we're just friends."

But then I told her, *"That's fine! That's okay! So long as you're around that's good enough for me."*

So for the next eight years I kept myself busy persistently pursuing my outer purpose. I attended every networking event I could find so that I could get my business card into the hands of decision makers. The hard work paid off in 2006 when I was contacted by NBC. They were looking for variety acts to perform on the first season of their new television show, *America's Got Talent*. I was so excited! Because I knew that that could be the big break I needed to move my career to the next level, by getting in front of a national audience.

So I picked my best magic trick, and hopped on a train for New York City. When I arrived at the audition I got into a line that wrapped around the block several times. And I waited, and I waited, and I waited — did I mention that patience is a big part of this idea? I waited a long time, and then the line was shut down, and the producers gave us all passes to go back the next day. But I never went back, because I had something more important that I needed to do that day.

Because I told Stephanie that I would drive her to the airport. Of course, I didn't tell Stephanie that I was missing the most important opportunity of my career; she would have refused my ride and forced me to go to the audition. But I wanted to drive her to the airport. I wanted to be there for her — because she was more important, than any audition, than any magic show ... she was more valuable.

I'm happy that I put by values in order, because a year later, in the summer of 2007, Stephanie came to me, and she said, *"Jonas, I'm in love with you too."*

It was the happiest day of my life.

We quickly became engaged to be married, and that weekend, Labor Day weekend, we went on vacation. She had never been on go-carts; twenty-six years old and she had never been on go-carts! So I took her on the go-carts. She had never been to a drive-in movie, so I took her to the drive-in. We went rock-wall climbing; we watched fireworks over Lake Winnipesauke. We smiled, and we laughed, and we danced. Oh my goodness we danced. And then, just two days after we got back from the most amazing weekend of our lives, in her sleep, she quietly passed away.

She just didn't wake up. Twenty-six years old, and there was no warning for her aneurism.

I thought I was going to die of a broken heart and, when I didn't, I turned to alcohol to do it for me.

I woke up one morning, about two years later, still half-drunk from the night before, and I found on my desk a perfectly typed suicide note that I had no memory of writing. If I could do something like that and not even know it, what else? ... I looked in the mirror that day and didn't recognize the man I had become.

I didn't want to live the life I was living anymore, but I knew I couldn't go back to be who I once was. I came to understand that even though I couldn't change what happened ... even though I couldn't leave the room ... I came to understand that what I could change was my perspective. I came to understand that I had to persist. Even though I couldn't see what it was anymore, I still had a purpose, so I had to keep on living, to grow to be more than I ever dreamed I could be.

I then realized that I had a choice, and we all have that same choice. The person we were yesterday doesn't have to be the person we are today, and the person we are today doesn't have to be the person we are tomorrow, especially if we've been playing a game of musical electric chairs.

What I'm suggesting is that we have a choice to live in the past, to live with the present, or to live for the future. It's okay to remember the past, and it's okay to dream of the future; but what's not okay is to let those dreams and remembrances rob us of the present moment, because this is all that we have.

I'm reminded of what happened to Puff when his friend Jackie Paper stopped coming around:

> *"Without his life-long friend, Puff could not be brave. So Puff, that mighty dragon, sadly slipped into his cave."*[32]

Puff was stuck comparing the way things used to be to the way that things turned out. He was no longer able to be happy because he couldn't see past the hurt of losing his friend. Puff had put his happiness "in a sand castle," to reference to an earlier example. But the happiness that Richard Kraut advocates for is goes beyond the temporary and fleeting, and, like Locke, suggests something more "true and solid."

I'm thinking of the kind of happiness that the Whos down in Whoville felt even after the Grinch stole Christmas.[33] We could argue using Bentham's hedonic calculus that the Whos could have experienced more pleasure had the Grinch *not* stolen Christmas, but that isn't necessary. The Whos placed their happiness inside a castle of stone where neither moth nor rust nor Grinches can steal it away.

---

[32] Peter, Paul and Mary. "Puff, The Magic Dragon." *Moving*, Warner Music Group. 1962

[33] Dr. Seuss. *How The Grinch Stole Christmas!* Random House, 1957

Perhaps the greatest reminder of this is our own mortality, because in the end no one is going to make it out alive, so it puts a fire under us to not waste our time, always keeping what's most important in the forefront.

Even Steve Jobs recognized this. He once said:

"Remembering that you're going to die is the best way I know to avoid the trap of thinking you have something to lose."[34]

So don't waste your time. Remember, you can just as easily fail at doing what you don't want to do, so why waste time living anything less than who you truly are? The comedian and actor Jim Carrey tells a poignant story of the importance of living a live that live sup to your standards of living:

"My father could have been a great comedian but he didn't believe that was possible for him. So he made a conservative choice. Instead, he got a safe job as an accountant and when I was 12 years old, he was let go from that safe job and our family had to do whatever we could to survive. I learned many great lessons from my father. Not the least of which was that you can fail at what you don't want, so you might as well take a chance on doing what you love."[35]

---

[34] Jobs, Steve. *Stanford University Commencement Address*. 2005
[35] Carrey, Jim. *Maharishi University of Management Commencement Address*, 2014

REFLECTIONS

1) *Have you been waiting to be happy? What are you waiting for?*

2) *What gift to the world are you sitting on?*

3) *What can you do today to be happy?*

4) *What are you willing to do to be satisfied with life?*

CHAPTER SIX

THE STRUCTURE OF HAPPINESS

"Please, don't worry so much. Because in the end, none of us have very long on this Earth. Life is fleeting ... Make your life spectacular."

— Jack Powell

THE STRUCTURE OF HAPPINESS

*T*his book has discussed a number of possible paths to take in the pursuit of happiness. Each path has alluring qualities, yet each path has their difficulties. I hope you have found this text useful in exploring your own understanding of happiness. What follows in this last section is my attempt to overcome those difficulties while maximizing the alluring qualities. The result is my own personal prescription for pursuing happiness, measured by my own application of the theories espoused by the philosophers discussed in this book.

It is my belief that the model discussed here is both objective and subjective, in that the structure is sound universally, yet must be applied to one's own life to be effective. I'd be fascinated to hear from you on your own application of this model should you choose to use it.

Enjoy!

INTRODUCTION

*T*he Structure of Happiness is supported by Four Pillars: *character, values, achievements, and gratitude.* Character refers to one's natural disposition (whether innate or learned); values refer to what one deems important based on their disposition; achievements refer to the things that one does based on their values (whether through disciplined or chance circumstances); and gratitude refers to exercising proper thoughts in relation to one's character, values, and achievements. What is revealing about this understanding of happiness is that though these Four Pillars are important to happiness, merely wanting and working towards obtaining them is not enough. Meaning, in seeking these Pillars there exist variables that are under one's control (character and values) as well as variable that are not (achievements). This is why cultivating the Fourth Pillar (of gratitude) is crucial. Three Pillars, even while less stable than four, are still sufficient for supporting the Structure of Happiness.

This manifesto will examine each of the Four Pillars of happiness in detail to demonstrate how each supports the overall Structure of Happiness. To illustrate a practical application of this theory I will write directly about my own character, values, achievements, and gratitude. The reader is encouraged to consider carefully these prescriptions and see how the theory is applicable to happiness universally.

THE FIRST PILLAR: CHARACTER

The First Pillar is made up of my personal character, both innate and learned. That is to say, my character is a combination of my natural tendencies, as well as my efforts to foster desired traits and to diminish undesirable traits. As it pertains to my Structure of Happiness, the character traits that I must master include being patient, forgiving, charitable, gracious, tenacious, humble, moderate, and trustworthy. It should be noted that while these are important traits to inculcate into my Being in order to be happy, they are never to be considered an end goal. That is to say, I must never be so daft as to presume myself to have a fully developed character in any category. For if complacency sets in I will cease to grow, and if I cease to grow I will stop moving forward, and if I stop moving forward I will begin to slide backwards, and if I slide backwards I will lose the character that I developed, and if I lose the character that I developed while holding the belief that I have already achieved forever such traits then I will live a lie, thus destroying the First Pillar. No matter how much progress has been made there will always be room to grow, forever finding new ways to express and reflect the character that I wish to Be.

THE SECOND PILLAR: VALUES

Based on my personal character, the Second Pillar is built with my values. The Structure of Happiness is *definably* a prescriptive edifice. As such, informing the decision-making process is a focus on my values. The question ever before me will be: *"What do I value?"* The follow-up question will always be: *"Based on those values, how should I respond to the circumstance before me?"* As of the Spring of 2016, these values include (in no particular order): living debt free; daily access to a safe and consistent shelter, safe and reliable transportation to and from my responsibilities; healthy and affordable food, clean and simple clothing that enables little alteration; maintaining a healthy lifestyle that promotes sound health for my body, mind, and emotions; maintaining as few possessions as possible; frequent opportunities for artistic expression; experiencing new and exciting places; and fostering meaningful relationships with loved ones; being of service to others, especially to emerging adults. These values can be expressed in a myriad of ways, and are certainly open to interpretation. Even from a personal perspective, how I interpret these values can vary depending on the circumstance. To be more precise I will detail each value in brief detail.

Living debt free: I value not owing anyone anything. This value will inform financial decisions and work ethics. I will not buy anything that I cannot afford to pay for in cash. I will work hard to obtain financial award enough to pay for anything that I may need. I will be frugal in my spending.

Daily access to a safe and consistent shelter: No matter where I find myself, I will value having a safe place to go. As such, I will accept nothing less than this. Consistency is key: this facet will ensure a long-term living situation, and likely require purchasing my own home.

Daily access to safe and reliable transportation to and from my responsibilities: the values I place on other things require work, and work that will require daily transportation in some form. This will likely turn out to be ownership of a small fuel-efficient automobile. In addition, this value also informs my actions; for example, it decides for me how I will care for whatever vehicle I obtain and dictates my driving habits.

Daily access to healthy and affordable food: healthy is key, for it will ensure that my body stays strong to tend to my duties, and affordable will also be key, to ensure that I can afford other necessities. This will likely play out to be a preplanned menu of meal options, which will cut down on shopping time and maximize time for other important activities, and make deviation from healthy eating less likely.

Daily access to clean and simple clothing that enables little alteration: This value has two key facets: that the clothes are clean, and that the clothes are predictable and able to be worn in multiple places, resulting in a smaller wardrobe. This will likely play out to be much like the clothes that I've been wearing for some time: affordable dress clothes that are durable. By only wearing dress clothes I will never be caught off guard by circumstances where formal wear is required. Best to be overdressed than underdressed; a necktie can be taken off if worn, but cannot be added if left at home. Also, by wearing the same clothes everyday I will spend far less time trying to determine what clothes to wear each day. These moments will add up to big time savings over a lifetime.

Maintaining a healthy lifestyle that promotes sound health for my body, mind, and emotions: this value relates to healthy eating. In order to do all that I am required to do in this life my body must be able to do these things. As such, I shall everyday include physical activity to maintain fitness; mental stimulation to stay sharp; and quiet reflection alone to maintain equanimity.

Maintaining as few possessions as possible: By eschewing material possessions I will be freed financially to only spend money on important matters, I will have a clean living space free of clutter, and I will be far freer by not being tied down by possessions.

Frequent opportunities for artistic expression: As a performance artists this is an important matter.

For while I do not intend to make this a primary source of income, it is important to my Being to exercise such talents. In fact, I'll go as far as to say that I would prefer to not rely on this for financial gain, for in my experience that has led only to despising such work.

Experiencing new and exciting places: This value is important to safeguard against stagnation. It is easy to get into a routine and succumb to monotony, for it is always far easier in the short term to keep things as they are rather than change, even if it is for the better in the long term. Exciting places include places that I've never been to, places that I rarely go to, historical places, landmarks, beautiful places, places that inspire awe. Best to not spend too much time in these places, though, for there must be time left to go other places and also still enough time to tend to my day-to-day responsibilities.

Fostering meaningful relationships with loved ones: This value is as much for my benefit as it is for the beloved. Is it very easy to get so caught up in day-to-day responsibilities that family and friends can get pushed to secondary concerns. But doing so is not good. As the philosopher Joe Cocker once said: "I get by with a little help from my friends." This is as much true for me as it is for the beloved. My friends and family get by with a little help from me, and as such I must make the cultivation of these relationships part of my day-to-day responsibilities.

85

Being of service to others, especially to emerging adults: This value lies at the core of many other values, acting as a foundational value. When in doubt of what to do, I will always err on the side of service to others. Most especially to young people. I get a profound sense of Joy from working with emerging adults, just leaving high school and entering college or the workforce. Every year for the past sixteen years I've volunteered for a youth leadership program and it has proven to be my most valuable work. I value this volunteer work over any paid work that I've ever done. As such, being of service to others will always be a core value.

THE THIRD PILLAR: ACHIEVEMENTS

Achievements come in three forms: they are the things that I *aim* to do, the things that I *do* do, and the things that I *did* do. Seeking achievements gives life motivation. Without such motivations there'd be little reason to get out of bed in the morning. This is evidenced by the fact that during periods of my life when I did not have an aim of purposeful achievements I'd too often slept my days away and, when I did rise, I'd remain cloistered in my apartment, often taking melatonin to resume sleeping. An idle life is meaningless and does not contribute to happiness; for this reason, desiring achievements inspired by my values is important for motivating participation with life and the world around me. Achievements are important for in-the-moment life satisfaction, for goals to look forward to, and are a source of pride in past accomplishments.

The achievements that I pull back my bow on today, and aim my arrow on the target of, are those things that express my values, now, in the past, and in the future. They include, for example, (to name just a few in no particular order): Obtain a graduate degree in Human Resources; live on half of my income, and save the rest for adventures and emergencies; buy an Escape Home;[36] continue my exercise regimen and book a guided excursion to a basecamp on Mount Everest;[37] consistently make weekly and monthly in-person and phone call visits with my core and extended family and friends; and book venues to perform my show *4000 Years Of Magic!* [38] These are but a few select achievements that I am currently seeking and, being based on my values, would be disappointing if any of them did not become accomplished.

Achievements are functional not only for adding motivation to life, but they also serve as a yardstick for measuring success. Having meaningful achievements signify that my life is going well, providing evidence that I am on the right track. Yet, equally important, failing to

---

[36] EscapeHomes.us
[37] NationalGeographicExpeditions.com
[38] JonasCain.com/4000Years

achieve my aims is another useful measure, for it will signify where I need to focus my energies for self-improvement. Key to the achievement pillar is striving to be a better man than I was; better than I was last year, last month, last week, yesterday, and even better than the man I was just a few moments ago. In this way, even when I inevitably fail, it will be looked upon as functional to my cultivation of happiness. But what happens when I fail again? What happens if certain aims that I've set out to achieve are never realized? What then? This is where the Fourth Pillar steps in to maintain happiness' stability.

THE FOURTH PILLAR: GRATITUDE

Formed by my character, values, and achievements, is the Fourth-Pillar-mortar of gratitude. You will recall that gratitude is a component of the First Pillar. Gratitude here, however, stands on its own in an evolved capacity. Character refers not only to how we interact with others, but also with how we interact with ourselves. The Fourth Pillar's understanding of gratitude is to maintain proper thoughts towards achievements, whether they have been successful or are failing. In my own life, this will be played out by carefully examining, each day, the achievements that have been pivotal to my happiness and verbalizing appreciation for the circumstances that led to the fulfillment of those aims. As for those aims that have as of yet failed, I must also express thanksgiving for the opportunity to perform the *action of seeking*, and examine the deficiencies of character and/or values that caused such failings or delays. Once recognized, a new aim must then be made to turn these newly found weaknesses into strengths. In instances of continued failure of important achievements, these too must be seen as welcomed guests to my experiences, for the proper-thinking under such a circumstance will be to see it as an opportunity to more fully appreciate the good aim that I do have in the other areas of my life. Sometimes Life says "no," and graciously accepting this answer is important to happiness. In this way, the Forth Pillar acts as a safety net for when any of the other three Pillars fail.

Another way of approaching the Fourth Pillar is to recognize that there are many ways to express character and values. Living by gratitude means acknowledging that achievements are not always in what *I plan* to do; it is an appreciation for what *life gives* in response to my actions.

CONCLUSION

By my personal examples we have seen how character, values, achievements, and gratitude support the Structure of Happiness. It is my hope that through these examples you have been able to see yourself reflected in the blueprint. If you find this manifesto un-useful then this may reveal two possibilities: (1) that this model is flawed, or, (2) that happiness, even in abstraction, is strictly relative. I propose that there is but one prescription for determining the functionality of this theory:

> *Three frogs sat on a log. One frog decided it was time to jump off the log and swim in the water. How many frogs remain on the log? You would think that there are now only two, yet in truth there remain three — for the frog who wanted to swim only <u>decided</u> that's what it wanted to do, yet never took the time to jump into action.*

A land called Hanalei

APPENDIX

*T*he following outline consists of suggestions for further independent study, including videos readily available on YouTube, as well as a number of reading selections from two books by Mulnix & Mulnix: *Theories of Happiness* (TOH), and *Happy Lives, Good Lives* (HLGL). My own personal understanding of happiness is heavily informed by my participation in a course taught by Dr. M.J. Mulnix at Salem State University entitled The Philosophy of Happiness. In your own pursuit of happiness you may find these sources helpful:

— Happiness As Pleasure —

Quantitative Hedonism
Jeremy Bentham: "Introduction to the Principles of Morals and Legislation"
(TOH pp. 21-26)

HLGL Chapter Four: "The Feel Good Feature of Happiness," pp. 61-71

Objective Hedonic Happiness
Daniel Kahneman: "Experienced Utility and Objective Happiness: A Moment Based Approach"
(TOH pp. 27-43)

HLGL Chapter Four: "The Feel Good Feature of Happiness," pp. 71-81

TED Talk: Daniel Kahneman: "The Riddle of Experience vs. Memory"

Qualitative Hedonism
John Stuart Mill: "Selections from Utilitarianism"
(TOH pp. 44-56)

HLGL Chapter Four: "The Feel Good Feature of Happiness,"
pp. 81-92.

Attitudinal Hedonism
Fred Feldman: "What is This Thing Called Happiness?"
(TOH pp. 57-80)

HLGL Chapter Five: "Taking Pleasure in Things and Feeling Joy," pp. 93-100.

The Problem of Miswanting
Daniel Gilbert: "Miswanting: Some Problems in the Forecasting of Future Affective States"
(TOH pp. 81-95)

HLGL Chapter Five: "Taking Pleasure in Things and Feeling Joy," pp. 100-106

TED Talk: Dan Gilbert: "The Surprising Science of Happiness"

Happiness Is Not A Transitory Episode
Daniel Haybron: "An Emotional State Account of Happiness"
(TOH pp. 96-113)

HLGL Chapter Five: "Taking Pleasure in Things and Feeling Joy," pp. 106-113

— Happiness As Satisfaction —

Happiness Is About Whole-Life – Not Simply Episodic.
Wladyslaw Tatarkiewicz: "Happiness and Time"
(TOH pp. 117-126)

HLGL Chapter Six: "Satisfied with What?" pp. 117-133

...and The Pursuit of Happiness

Problems With Life Satisfaction Judgments

HLGL Chapter Six: "Satisfied with What?" pp. 133-145

TED Talk: Barry Schwartz: "The Paradox of Choice"

Values & Non-Arbitrary Judgments of Life Satisfaction

Valerie Tiberius and Alicia Hall: "Normative Theory and Psychological Research: Hedonism, Eudaimonism, and Why It Matters"
(TOH pp. 127-151)

HLGL Chapter Seven: "It's All about Perspective," pp. 146-156

Not Just Any Old Want Counts

John Kekes: "Happiness"
(TOH pp. 152-169)

HLGL Chapter Seven: "It's All about Perspective," pp. 156-172

What Psychologists Can Teach Politicians

Ed Diener and Martin Seligman: "Beyond Money: Toward an Economy of Well-Being"
(TOH pp. 170-218)

TED Talk: Michael Norton: "How to Buy Happiness"

TED Talk: Martin Seligman: "The New Era of Positive Psychology"

Worries with the Economy of Happiness

Martha Nussbaum: "Who's the Happy Warrior?: Philosophy, Happiness Research, and Public Policy"
(TOH pp. 219-245)

Social Science and the Tyranny of the Majority

John Stuart Mill: "On Liberty" Chapter 3

The Greatest Happiness for the Greatest Number?

HLGL Chapter 11: "Justice and National Happiness" pp. 265-297.

Video: Mulnix and Mulnix: "Justice and National Well-Being."

Are Subjective Experiences really all that matter?
Robert Nozick: "Happiness"
(TOH pp. 246-262)

HLGL Chapter 8: "Is Ignorance Bliss?" pp. 175-184

— Happiness As Eudemonia —

Happiness, Experience Machine, Deception, & Achievement
HLGL Chapter 8: "Is Ignorance Bliss?" pp. 185-196

Julia Annas: "Happiness and Achievement"

Happiness as Inner Harmony
Plato: "Selections from Republic"
(TOH pp. 265-300)

HLGL Chapter 9: "Happiness, Moral Virtue, and the Purpose of Life," pp. 197-213)

Plato: "Selections from Republic"
(TOH pp. 265-300)

HLGL Chapter 9: "Happiness, Moral Virtue, and the Purpose of Life," pp. 197-213

A Life That Lacks Nothing
Aristotle: "Selections from Nicomachean Ethics"
(TOH pp. 320-355)

HLGL Chapter 9: "Happiness, Moral Virtue, and the Purpose of Life," pp. 213-226

Aristotle: "Selections from Nicomachean Ethics"
(TOH pp. 320-355)

HLGL Chapter 9: "Happiness, Moral Virtue, and the Purpose of Life," pp. 213-226

Happiness or Well-Being? & How Much is Enough?
Richard Kraut: "Two Conceptions of Happiness"
(TOH pp. 356-381)

HLGL Chapter 9: "Happiness, Moral Virtue, and the Purpose of Life," pp. 226-231.

Epictetus: "The Handbook of Epictetus"

Epictetus: "The Handbook of Epictetus"

Buddhism
Dalai Lama: "Selections from The Art of Happiness"
(TOH pp. 407-429)

TED Talk: Matthieu Ricard: "The Habits of Happiness"

Finding Happiness Even In Suffering
HLGL Chapter 10: "Finding Equanimity in the Face of Suffering," pp. 232-262.

TED Talk: Mihaly Cskiszentmihalyi: "Flow, the Secret to Happiness"

BOOKS BY JONAS CAIN

It Just Happened The Other Day:
A True Story

One day two best friends decided to write a book together. Before a word was even written they already had a title for it. Whenever Stephanie told a story she would begin by saying, "It just happened the other day," even if it had actually happened months earlier; and whenever Jonas told a story he would begin by saying, "It's a true story," even when what he was saying was actually a joke. Due to unforeseen circumstances, the pair never got to write their book...until now.

A poignant true story of love, loss, and inspired hope, It Just Happened the Other Day: A True Story is sure to touch the heart of all readers.

Just Another Day

The long awaited sequel to It Just Happened the Other Day: A True Story, this book opens on just another day for Jonas Cain as he embarks on a cross-country bicycle ride, from MA to L.A. Detailing his ensuing detours, this book highlights that the actual destination truly matters little when you're on an adventure.

Journey Of Discovery:
Awaken Your Inner Power

A book you can read in an hour or keep on your nightstand for daily inspiration, Journey of Discovery: Awaken Your Inner Power offers concise practical ideas for bringing your inner purpose to Light. If approached with an open heart and an honest mind, this material is sure to help you on your journey to awaken your inner power.

And The Pursuit Of Happiness

In the Declaration of Independence Thomas Jefferson wrote:

> *"We hold these truths to be self-evident, that all men are created equal, that they are endowed by their Creator with certain unalienable Rights, that among these are Life, Liberty and the pursuit of Happiness."*

Assuming that this statement is true the question becomes: What exactly is this "happiness" that we have a fundamental right to pursue?

The Problem Of Poverty

By examining the individual and structural causes of poverty, and the political, religious, and ethical perspectives of society's obligation to the poor, this preliminary study aims to suggest an innovative course of action to deal with this social problem. This proposed prescription will have a focused emphasis on individual responsibility implemented in pockets of localized communities that when duplicated across regions will demonstrate significant national success.

Absurd Jokes

Inspired by the time Jonas figured out the meaning of the term Pittsburgh Steelers, after being mugged on the streets of Pittsburgh, this book suggests a mathematical equation for humor:

$$tragedy + time = humor$$

This edited compilation of Jonas Cain's all-time favorite jokes aims to offer readers inspiration to find solace in the humor of life's tragedies.

Magic Words

Leveraging his over twenty-year career as a magician, *Magic Words* is Jonas Cain's tome of over 52 Magic Words presented and explained to help readers quickly and easily implement these words into their daily lives to conjure personal and professional growth. Read it straight through cover-to-cover, or keep it on your nightstand for daily encouragement, either way *Magic Words* will engage and empower you to Boldly Step Forward PERFORM!

Are You P.O.S.I.T.I.V.E.?

Positivity is often misunderstood to mean putting on a pair of rose-colored glasses, pretending that everything is fine and dandy, even when everything isn't fine and dandy. But Jonas Cain holds that this understanding of positivity is flawed, arguing that true positivity can not ignore reality but instead has to reflect an honest assessment of the truth.

Are Your P.O.S.I.T.I.V.E.? will take you on an 8-step journey that will encourage you to "rethink positive thinking," opening you to a life of engagement and empowerment!

ABOUT THE AUTHOR

Jonas Cain is a positivity expert, author, magician, and corporate trainer. For over twenty years he has sought to engage, empower, and encourage others to become Positivity Leaders at home, work, and within the community.

Through his interactive keynote presentations, motivational magic performances, and engaging training workshops, Jonas has worked with major corporations, organizations, universities, sporting teams, military installations, and countless individuals, sharing research, tools, and strategies for developing and fostering positivity in all areas of life.

For complete information on his programs, or if you'd like to invite Jonas to speak with your group, visit:

www.JonasCain.com